AF248650

Noarm 1985-86, mixed media, 45 x 16 x 8 1/2 inches

PETER SHELTON

WAXWORKS

DES MOINES ART CENTER

ACKNOWLEDGMENTS
Julia Brown Turrell, Director

It is a great pleasure to present the work of Peter Shelton at the Des Moines Art Center. I have long been an admirer of his sculpture and have watched its development over the last five years with great appreciation. Shelton's involvement with and manipulation of his materials, and his capacity to draw reference to human anatomy and movement in an inanimate object, create a compelling tension between abstraction and representation and result in powerful and enigmatic works of art. This exhibition explores the period between 1983 and 1988 and concentrates on Shelton's sculptural objects rather than his architectural environments which are also widely respected.

We have a number of people to thank for the successful organization of this exhibition and its catalogue. Connie Butler, Associate Curator of the Art Center curated the exhibition and produced and wrote its catalogue. Kimberly Davis and Peter Goulds of L.A. Louver gallery were extremely helpful in all phases of this project; and Christopher Munoz, Art Center intern, has been of great assistance in exhibition organization. Tory Pomeroy has beautifully installed the exhibition and Margaret Willard, Registrar, successfully handled all details of packing and shipping. On behalf of the artist we thank Catherine MacLean and Walter Woods for their invaluable assistance in fabrication of the work. We also thank the entire Art Center staff who is responsible for creating the artistic and administrative environment that allows these projects to be realized. I thank the Board of Trustees of the Art Center in particular, whose vision and committment to this institution and its programs has created a history and present state of excellence and ambition.

We are so pleased to share this exhibition with the La Jolla Museum of Contemporary Art and I extend special thanks to my colleague Hugh Davies, Director, for his participation in this project. We appreciate the generous assistance of Sue K. and Charles C. Edwards in the presentation of this exhibition in La Jolla. We gratefully acknowledge the generosity of all the lenders whose participation has made both exhibitions possible.

Lastly we extend all our special thanks to the artist, whose sculpture graces our museum and whose work is a constant source of pleasure and great interest.

This exhibition is funded through the generous support of the Anna K. Meredith Endowment Fund and the Lannan Foundation.

INTRODUCTION
Cornelia H. Butler, Curator

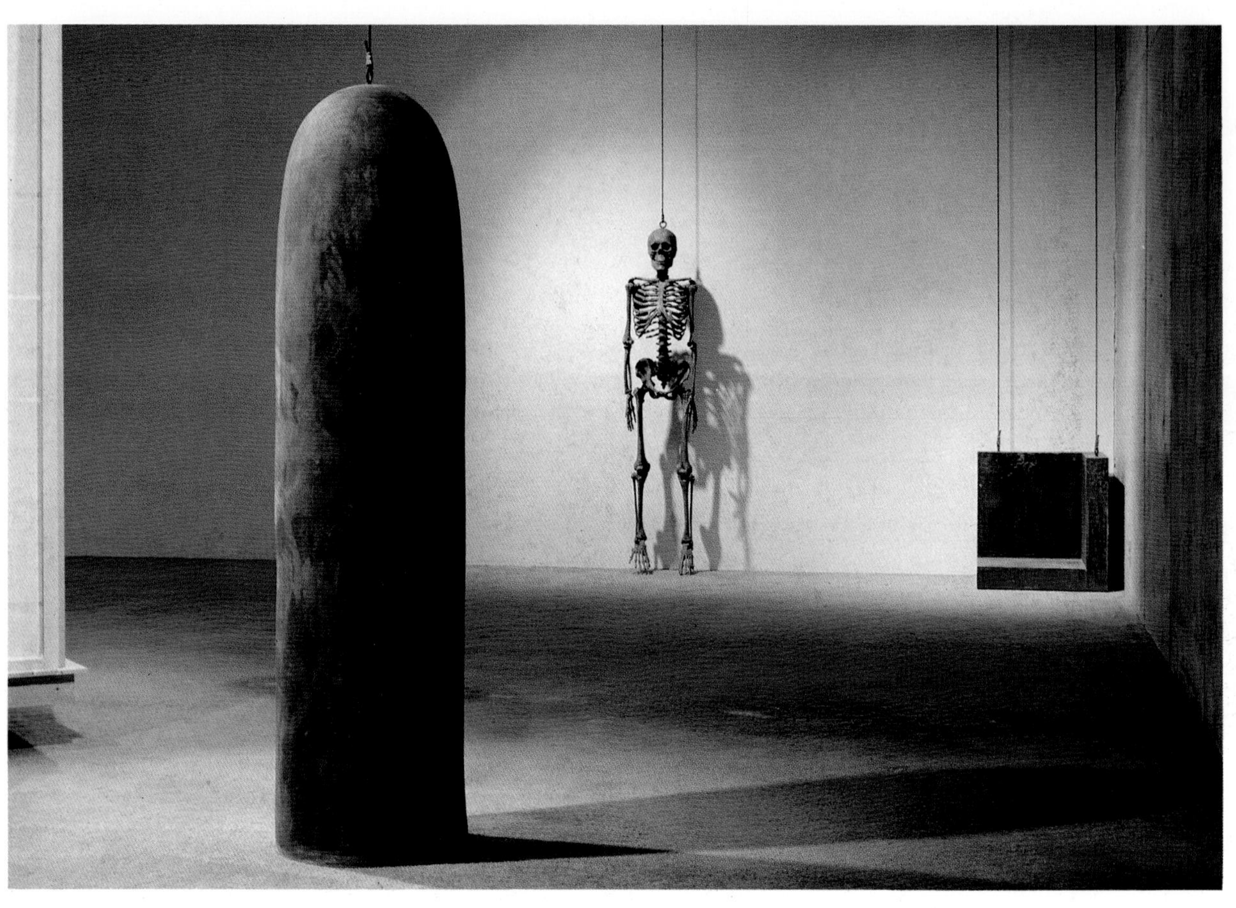

floatinghouse DEADMAN, 1985-86
detail *bbell*, cast iron, 66 x 16 inch diameter
detail *bones*, cast steel, 66 x 16 x 12 inches
detail *heavycorner*, steel, 24 x 24 x 24 inches

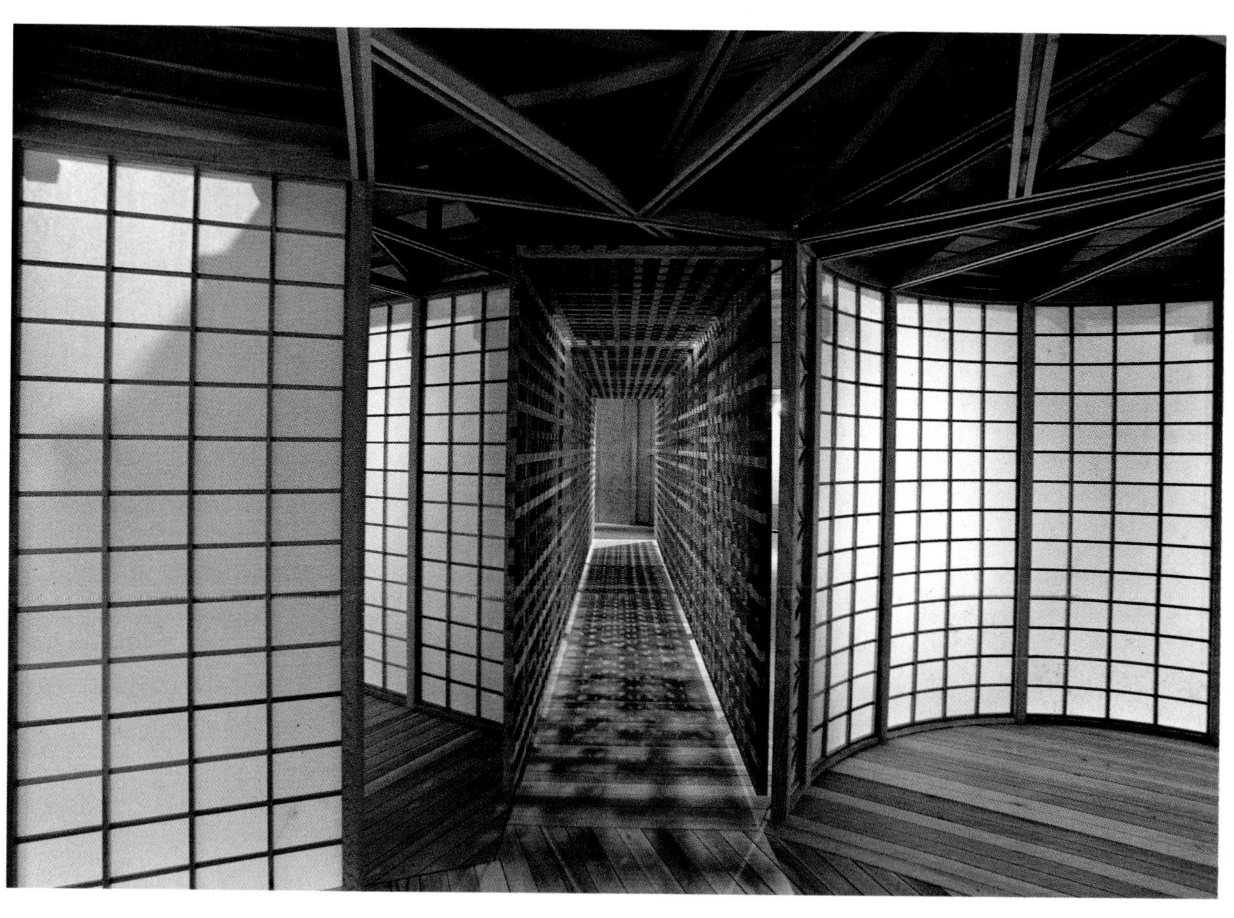

floatinghouse DEADMAN, 1985-86
interior of *floatinghouse* installation

WAXWORKS

The first time I spoke to Peter Shelton about his work he said, "One pill makes you big, one pill makes you small." The reference to *Alice in Wonderland* escaped me until I began to understand that this particular group of works, though perhaps the most approachable as three dimensional objects for visual appreciation, demand a physical attention as well. They engage us in conversation and insist on a heightened awareness of the relationship of our own bodies to the fiberglass, iron or bronze bodies which extend out from the wall, hang from the ceiling and glide along the floor. I thank Peter Shelton for pushing me down the *garden hole* and for the wonderful experience of gathering these objects which are to him, and now to all of us, such an important part of his work as an artist.

> *"Curiouser and curiouser!" cried Alice (she was so much surprised, that for the moment she quite forgot how to speak good English). "Now I'm opening out like the largest telescope that ever was! Good-bye, feet!" (for when she looked down at her feet, they seemed to be almost out of sight, they were getting so far off). "Oh, my poor little feet,...I shall be a great deal too far off to trouble myself about you: you must manage the best way you can – but I must be kind to them," thought Alice, "or perhaps they wo'n't walk the way I want to go!"*

When a tree falls in the forest, is there any sound with no one to listen? What is the sound of one hand clapping? What is the feeling of vertigo that comes from intoxication? How is it possible that an amputee continues to experience sensation in a phantom limb as if the body were whole, or that when we suffer a pain in one area of the body, another seemingly unrelated part twinges as well? And what is the disturbing sensation when we look into a surface which we thought would hold our reflection only to find the cabinet open or the window broken? For an instant we, like Alice, are missing, invisible or disembodied somehow. For a brief moment our physical frame of reference is radically altered or even jeopardized. What Alice experiences in Wonderland is not only the perversion of logic in an enchanted land where, if serpents eat eggs and little girls eat eggs, then little girls must be serpents, but also a radical alteration of the fragile hierarchy that makes up our physical being. As her neck stretches away from her shoulders and up through the trees, Alice wonders who will take care of her "poor little feet." They become things separate from her and, as they do, Alice begins to address herself as if she has been split into two separate people, her words and exclamations becoming in-creasingly twisted and childlike.

The unpredictability of Alice's deceptively innocent world is fundamentally related to the experience of Peter Shelton's installations and sculpture. The disparity between empirical and experienced reality and the constantly chang-ing, often ambiguous relationship between one's own body and external forces, is precisely that which makes Shelton's work challenging and enigmatic. His objects have a strong presence and yet exert a certain undeniable force on the experience of the viewer – a force that is not only visual but quite physical as well.

What are these strange objects that hang, float, jutt, poke, expand, contract and slide? At first glance there is a blue arm that projects out from the wall, a simple, clear tube that hovers horizontally, a black shirt with outstretched arms, and a set of quirky bronze shapes that resemble teeth. Some mimic human body parts in a rather literal way and others are generalized forms whose anthropomorphic roots one only senses. In fact, all of the sculptures inhabiting the room are about, though not contingent upon, presence – the longer we remain the more we are made acutely aware of our own physical existence in relation to the air, space, light, dimensions that constitute our environment.

The operation of Shelton's titles, and his preoccupation with the mechanism of language in general, can be read as a metaphor for the convoluted almost incestuous way his work evolves, and for the peculiar way these objects relate to one another. In much the same way that Lewis Carroll's childhood fairy tale is actually a complex allegory filled with phenomenological twists and permutations of language, so too are Shelton's objects not what they first appear. Beginning with the titles, it is quickly apparent that, like the *"waxworks"* themselves, some are mundane and descriptive (*Bluearm ,
Simplecleartube, Sleepwalker*) while some are more enigmatic and poetic (*Noarm, Twoarmstoolong, Pins*). In reference to Duchamp's film "Anemic Cinema" Tobey Mussman states that "...puns, unlike ordinary sentences, do not attempt to make a definite statement but rather they cast ironic doubt on the ability of any written sentence to make ultimate and absolute sense."[1] In nearly all cases the words in Shelton's titles have been allowed to run together, yielding odd combinations of vowels and consonants which create new words or puns such as *32th*. I am reminded of the childhood wordgame of words repeated over and over until the meaning not only fades but the sounds either take on new shape or congeal into a formless blob, empty of meaning and reference. The artist himself recalls afternoons spent fishing when he would literally hypnotize himself by mentally focusing on one word as a sort of mantra. In the same way that Alice has momentary lapses in coherence, which correspond in extremity to the metamorphoses of her bodily state, or the way the words and phrases that constitute the more poetic passages in the story are rhythmically divided and punctuated so that odd syllables are isolated or accented, so too do titles such as *Noarm, Facein* and *Twoarmstoolong* function as strange poetic hybrids in which

1.   Tobey Mussman, "Marcel Duchamp's Anemic Cinema," (1961) Reprinted in *The New American Cinema*, ed. Gregory Battcock (New York: E.P. Dutton and Co. Inc., 1967) p. 151.

the familiar becomes confusing and the generic is disrupted.

It is this kind of transformation and distortion that interests Shelton or, as he might put it, "the absolute absurdity of looking at someone so long that their face becomes quite ludicrous." Edges fade, features blend and, like the units of letters that comprise Shelton's titles, the hierarchy dissolves and reconstitutes. Shelton refers to the weight of language in his distribution of the upper and lower case letters in his titles and, as we will see, the way he plays with the relative importance of a syllable is really analogous to the variations in weight, shape and material in his small-scale objects. The parallel with language is as central to Shelton's work as it is to Alice's confusion.

In addressing the question of how the vocabulary of this body of work overlaps and underscores the rest of Shelton's enterprise we must look back to several earlier installations. It is, in fact, no easy task to discuss the progression of this artists's work in a linear way – the objects in this exhibition are intimately involved with issues first explored in larger works such as *HEADROOM footspace* (1980). In the catalogue of his recent exhibition at the Wight Gallery at the University of California, Los Angeles, Shelton describes one of his most important early works:

> *HEADROOM footspace* stacks two rooms one on top of the other. The floor of the lower, *HEAD-ROOM*, is five feet below grade and is entered by two stairways on opposite sides. A one-foot-wide open band puts your head on the ground amongst the grass, weeds and at the feet of people on the outside. The earth is no longer an abstract plane but is fragrant, densely packed matter. The feet of people in the room above are resting on your head.
>
> *Footspace* has proportions like the room below but one is instead contained from above. The room

floats above the floor with one's feet in the breeze of
the open band at the wall's bottom. Like the dinger
in a bell, one's lower body is strangely unattached.
Feet touch heads below. The tree grows upside down.[2]

The poetic way in which Shelton describes the experience
of standing or seeming to levitate in the hollow space of
HEADROOM footspace reveals much of the philosophy behind
his work. Strangely detached or disembodied, limbs are isolated
and individual sensations, normally undifferentiated and taken
for granted, are separated out and made the focal points of a new
experience. The zones usually allotted to very specific body parts
such as head and feet are reversed: eyes look out from underneath the structure at the horizontal expanse of ground, now at
eye level, while at the same time legs walking on the floor above
are experiencing the airiness usually reserved for the head. One
might say, a light-headedness of the feet. The body is the locus of
weightlessness, and gravity is now merely one force among many
instead of the referent.

In postulating the terms of our physical relationship
to objects and external forces such as gravity, and specifically the
physiological condition of the phantom limb, Merleau Ponty
states...

> The body is the vehicle of being in the world,
> and having a body is, for a living creature, to be inter-
> volved in a definite environment...I am conscious of
> the world through the medium of my body.
>
> To the extent that I have 'sense organs,' and a
> 'body,' and 'psychic functions,'...each of the moments
> of my experience ceases to be an integrated and
> strictly unique totality, in which details exist only in
> virtue of the whole; I become the meeting point of a
> host of 'casualties.'[3]

---

2.   Peter Shelton quoted in *floatinghouse DEADMAN* exhibition catalogue, Wight Art
Gallery, University of California, Los Angeles, 1987, p. 8.

3.   M. Merleau Ponty, Colon Smith trans., *Phenomenology of Perception* (New Jersey: The
Humanities press, 1962) pp. 82-83.

Ponty's *Phenomenology of Perception* was central to the practice of Minimalist sculptors of the sixties to whom Shelton is indebted. His definition of the body as a sensory repository in the world represents the philosophical parallel to Shelton's work. The ambiguity surrounding what Ponty describes as the two layers of human self-awareness, the habitual body or memoried body which is opposed to the situation of the body at a particular moment in time, is precisely where the tension lies in much of Shelton's architectural/sculptural installations. The way we are conditioned to perceive ourselves in space as beings bound and defined by the laws of gravity is, quite literally, turned upside down in works such as *HEADROOM footspace*.

Like Joel Shapiro, Bruce Nauman and several other sculptors with whom he identifies, Shelton's relationship to Minimalism is complicated. Formally the objects in this exhibition in particular are more closely aligned to such predecessors as Alberto Giacommetti and Louise Bourgeois and the erotic objects of Duchamp. Shelton's understanding of space and environment as material is related in many ways to the work of environmental artists Robert Irwin and James Turrell, with whom Shelton studied for a brief time at Pomona College , and whose work in the early seventies in California investigated spatial density and the physicality of light. In *BIRDHOUSE holecan* (1980) for example, a particularly interesting earlier work of Shelton's, *holecan* is a 72-inch tall cylinder which is perforated by 700 small holes which give the effect of dissolving the steel walls by letting in tiny shafts of light. The holes map the bodies of 25 of the artist's immediate family members. Says Shelton of this work, "One is alone in the *holecan* but there is an unexpected physical and social extension to the space."[4]

However, Shelton's greatest response to Minimalism is his consideration of weight, presence and interior space. In Michael Fried's now famous attack on Minimalism, it was these three characteristics which he posited as constituting the

---

4.   *floatinghouse DEADMAN* exhibition catalogue, Wight Art Gallery, University of California, Los Angeles, 1987, p. 9.

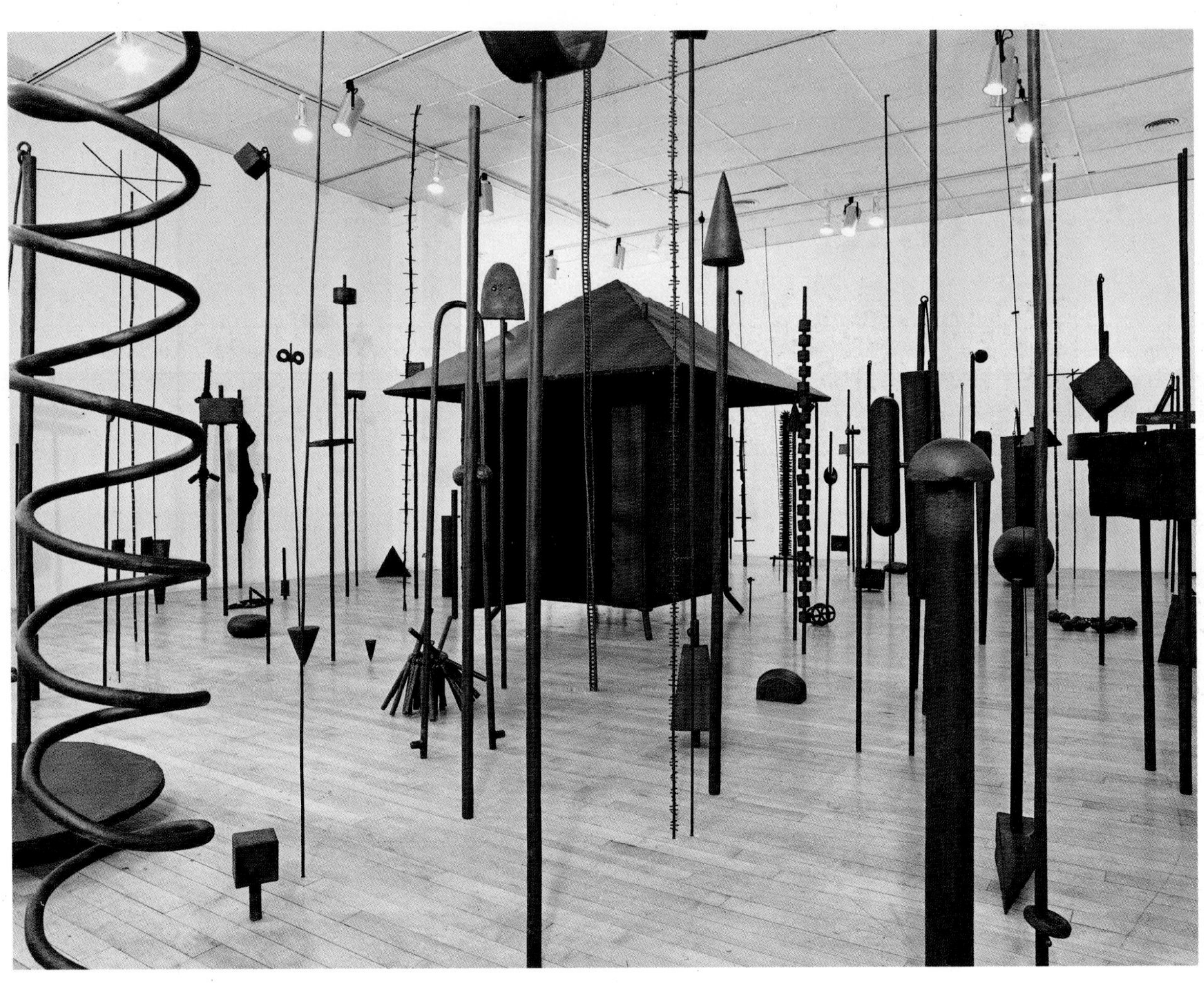

SWEATHOUSE and little principals 1977-82, steel
Contemporary Arts Forum, Santa Barbara, California

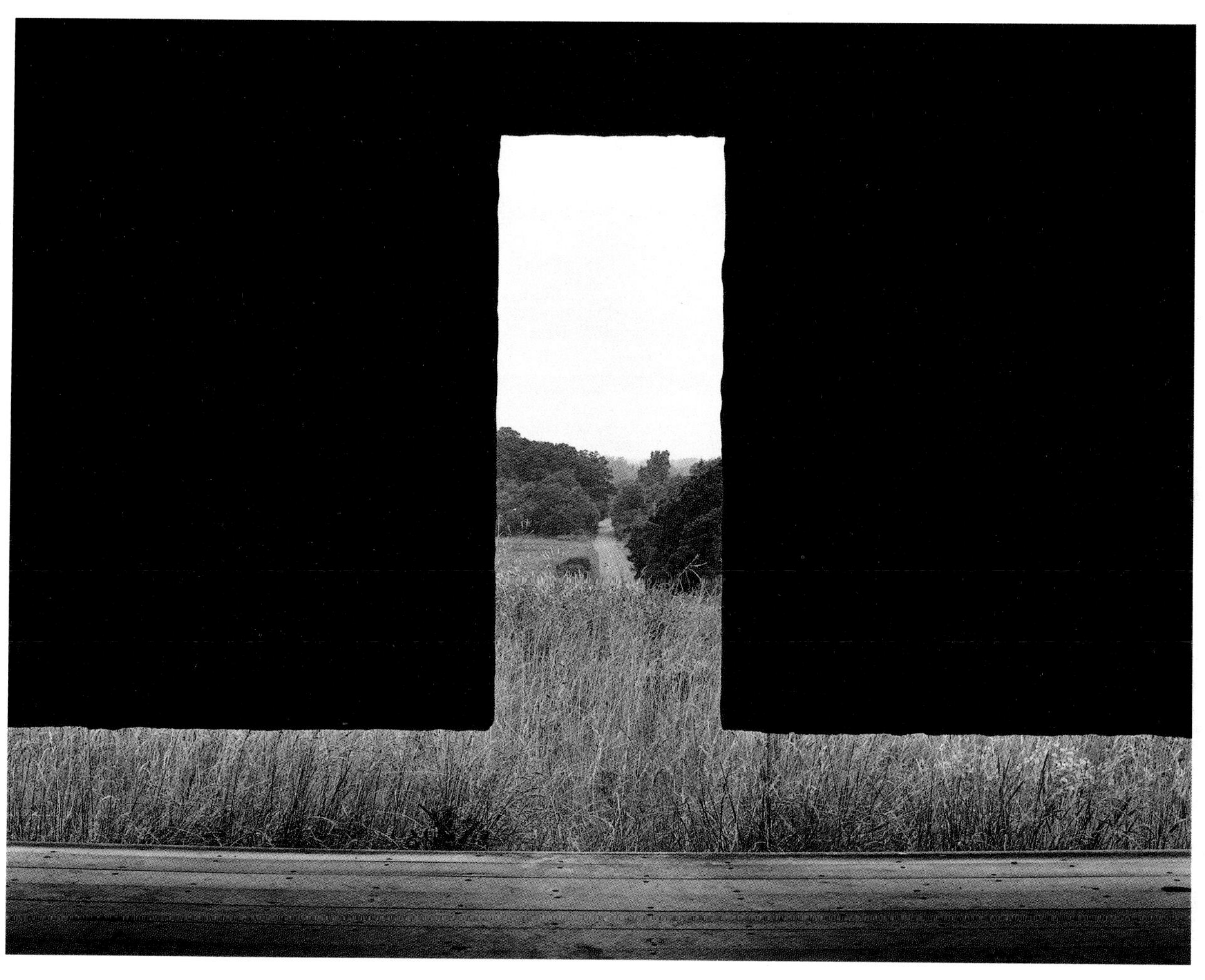

HEADROOM *footspace* 1980, steel, wood, cement
Artpark, Lewiston, New York

deplorable theatricality of Minimalist sculpture.[5] It was his contention that the problem with what he called Literalist art was its dependence on the presence of a viewer, and hence its theatricality. Furthermore, Fried asserted that the hollowness of much of the sculpture and the artists' concern over how the size and weight of an object might relate to and effect the viewer was, in fact, a veiled anthropomorphism or "latent or hidden naturalism."[6] And it was precisely these concerns that spawned the formal reaction against Minimalism in the work of such artists as Bruce Nauman, Joel Shapiro and Peter Shelton in the seventies. The radical schism created by the Minimalists paved the way for a new generation of sculptors whose task it became to reinvest the art object itself with a human content. In Bruce Nauman's work the injection was quite literal and took the form of autobiography – body as subject and material. Joel Shapiro initially chose to make his subject the theatricality or presentness of Minimal sculpture. His installations of tiny bronze objects – a coffin, bridge, bird or ladder – focused on the viewer as subject by upsetting the conventional notions of scale, space and weight in sculpture. His aim was to heighten the viewer's awareness of individual senses in relation to the objects on the floor: "the smallness denies the viewer a sense of completely shared space...provokes a mildly disembodied experience."[7]

Shelton's work is most closely allied with this body of Shapiro's early sculptures. As a post-Minimal sculptor his work shares these concerns in particular, but is especially rich because of the way issues of interiority or interior space, weight, presence and physical forces are humanized even further. The installations are not only about experience in a phenomenological way but they are infused with it. They describe it and are described by it.

There are two distinct groups of Shelton's earlier work which provide the impetus for the works in the current exhibition. *SWEATHOUSE and little principals* (1977-82), which the artist describes as analogous to a writer's first novel in terms of

<hr>

5. Michael Fried, "Art and Objecthood," reprinted in *Minimal Art: A Critical Anthology*, ed. Gregory Battcock (New York: E.P. Dutton and Co. Inc., 1968) pp. 116-147.

6. *Ibid.*, p. 129.

7. *Joel Shapiro*, Sculpture and drawing exhibition catalogue, Whitechapel Art Gallery, London, 1980; essay by Roberts Smith, p. 10.

its importance, was an installation of steel elements which were actually the sculptural working out of ideas logged in Shelton's sketch books. These books contain a bank of images which find physical form not only in the earlier installations, but in *Waxworks*. The objects in *SWEATHOUSE* were primarily vertical and relate to actual body parts in a very specific way. As one might guess, *Eyesballs,* a work quite similar to one in this installation, consists of two eye holes at the top of a hanging rod and two balls about halfway to the ground which correspond to the actual level of the artist's eyes and groin area. Thus the works address the viewer more literally than do Shapiro's early bronze objects. In fact, they are the most literal or particular of Shelton's sculpture. What becomes an erotic or at least voluptuous sensuality in the *Waxworks* is here a quirky, unrefined expression of physical form. Speaking about sculpture in general, Shelton has said,

> What makes sculpture strong is that it deals in the most physical way with the least physical of things – ideas. It is at once felt and graphic. Living in a body that eats, sleeps, defecates, reproduces and dies, and yet is full or soaring imagination, evolved concepts, and strong emotions is our concrete experience of this tension and connection.[8]

Given this description, I think it is fair to recall the fact that for many years Shelton wanted to be a doctor and was fascinated by the structure of the body and the particular conditions which effect the behavior of muscle groups and bones. One might say this is the concrete side of his philosophy of art-making – or, as he has expressed it, "the reconciliation of the self with space and with the frailty of the body."[9] The excitement in *MAJORJOINTS hangers and squat* and, to a much greater extent in *Waxworks*, is the abstraction of this primary physicality. After all, when Alice drinks the potion for the first time it is

8.   *floatinghouse DEADMAN* exhibition catalogue, Wight Art Gallery, University of California, Los Angeles, 1987, p. 24.

9.   Conversation with the artist, April 11, 1988.

not her shrinking size she worries about, but rather she revels in
the curious feeling of shutting up like a telescope or "going out
altogether like a candle."

The *floatinghouse DEADMAN* installation (1987) is the
culmination of all Shelton's previous works and contains elements
of each sculptural or environmental investigation. The exhibition
contains a cast steel skeleton, an iron chair, two large, cast iron
feet which resemble oversized clogs, a giant hammer, a steel bed
perforated with holes, a corner of steel and a pile of steel A's and
H's. All of these elements are counterweights to a large, suspended
house structure made of paper and wood. The anthropomorphic
floor plan is based on the configuration of Shelton's outstretched
body, and the paper exterior is a surrogate skin stretched around
the architectural skeleton. The *floatinghouse* is literally and figura-
tively countered by a small, steel model of a house which is sunken
in a steel box filled with water. Hence the miniature structure,
which possesses great weight and dead presence, helps support the
floating, human-scale structure which seems to have no weight.
Again the vocabulary is reversed and the normal is replaced by the
unexpected. Words take on new meaning.

This idea of a dialogue between the objects, the exploration
of interior versus exterior, the juxtaposition between bodies and
attenuated forms covered with a shell of skin – all of these bear on
the objects at hand. Whether literal or abstracted, *Waxworks* contains sculptures that Shelton himself views as three dimensional
sketches. They relate to memory in terms of our response to them.
In the context of Shelton's overall body of work they function as a
catalogue or inventory of working moulds. They are, in this sense,
waxworks or effigies of earlier ideas. The way wax is molded and
transformed by heat and other processes is analogous to the meta-
morphosis undergone by Shelton's ideas and his sculptural forms.
Several objects in the exhibition, *Twoarmstoolong, Gooseneck* and
Clearbelly, for example, are all forms which have been executed in
several different media. Thus there is a fluidity between the objects
and each other and, the way they activate the gallery walls and
space as fiberglass, iron or bronze objects. The different surfaces
and materials alter the way each work relates to the wall, ceiling or

floor. The fiberglass objects, for example, read as three-dimensional forms which inhabit and mischievously intrude on painting's domain. And yet they innervate the space with movement and completely disrupt the two-dimensional realm – "...using the space of paintings in which to float your sculpture."[10] The powerful phenomenon of weight felt in the cast, hanging sculpture is virtually absent from the wall works, which give the illusion of requiring no support at all.

There exists a curious range of sensation from the most specific to the most general not only in terms of the variations in the literal weight of the sculptures in this exhibition, but in terms of their color, surface, texture and engagement with interior versus exterior human space. Shelton's *Waxworks* are sensuous or even erotic in the same way as a soft sculpture by Claes Oldenburg appeals tactily to our senses or, one of Marcel Duchamp's erotic objects is not specifically erogenous so much as in the generalized treatment of forms and surfaces. *Redleft* is membranous and recalls the inner walls of arteries. It, quite literally, turns the other sculptures inside out. *Browntop* carries a variety of associations from the top of a bald head to the sphere of a pregnant stomach. *32th* is as much a battery of teeth as it is a collection of genitalia. *Greybone* is a body made of cellular tissue. In each of these, and equally in the cast iron works, interior or underneath are as important as on top or on the surface.

The artist's own description of what happens to us as we confront and interact with these works is, in the end, most accurate. We walk into an installation and respond to it as a generalized space which holds materially dense focii. As we adjust, the focal points, the sculptures, shift and associative forms begin to surface from memory and our physical frame of reference. Forms that start off as a seed, become something else later so that we begin to understand the essential nature of the objects and their strange relationship to our presence. These objects that are theatrical, architectural and sculptural all at once, have a curious effect on our perception. Edges fade, bodies metamorphose and we are reminded that "Wax-works weren't made to be looked at for nothing."[11]

10.   *Ibid.*
11.   Lewis Carroll, ed. Roger Lancelyn Green, *Alice's Adventures in Wonderland and Through the Looking-glass* (New York: Oxford University Press, 1986) p. 157.

PLATES

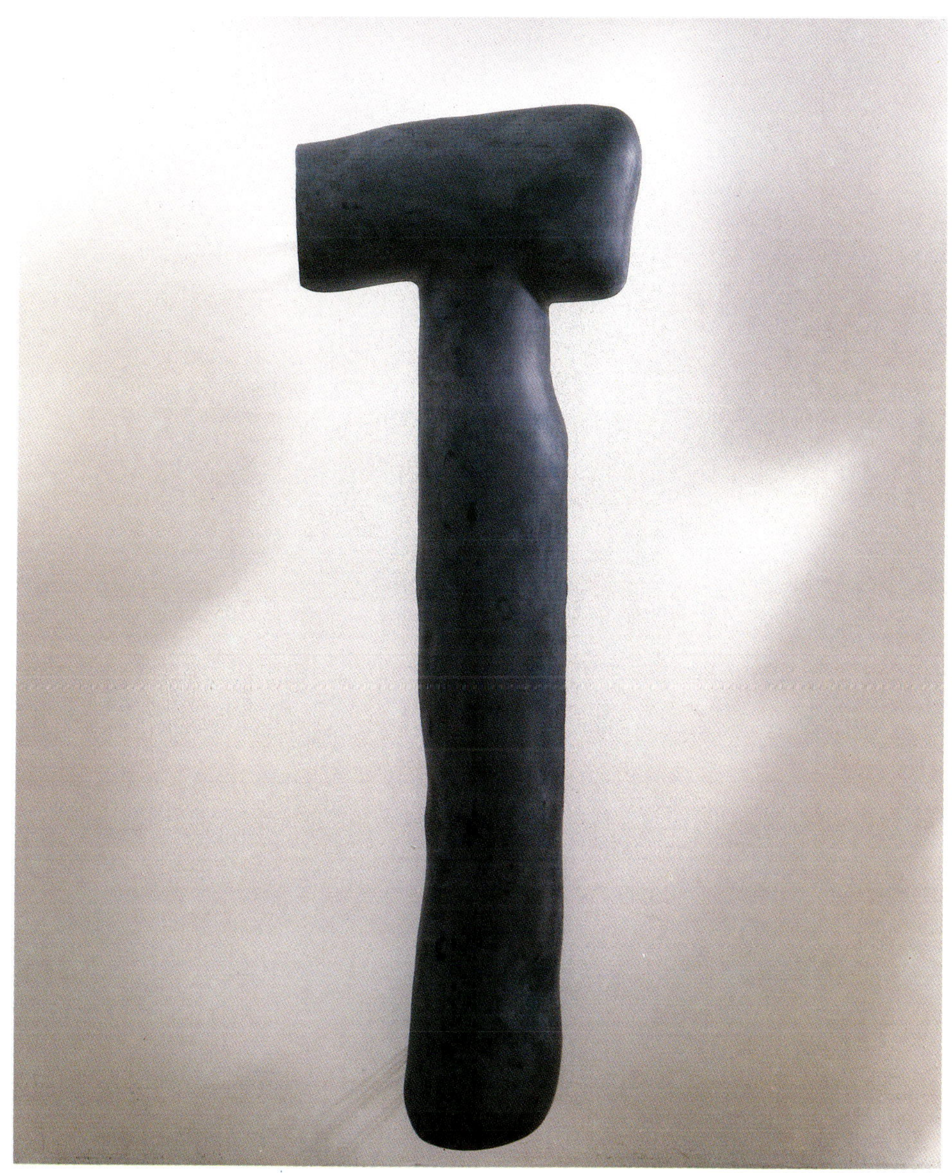

Hammerhead 1984-86, mixed media, 63 x 21 x 9 inches

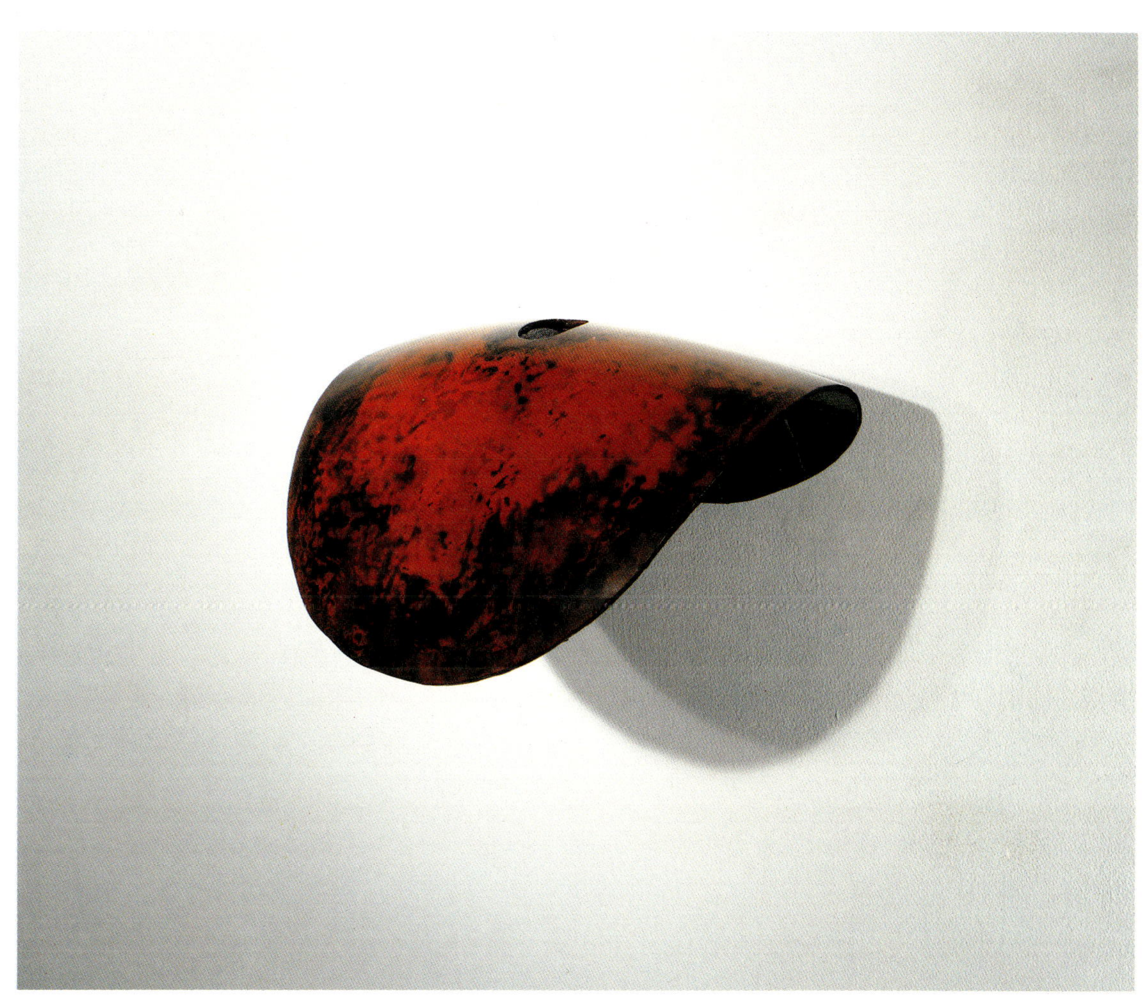

Redmantle 1984-86, mixed media, 9 x 16 1/2 inches

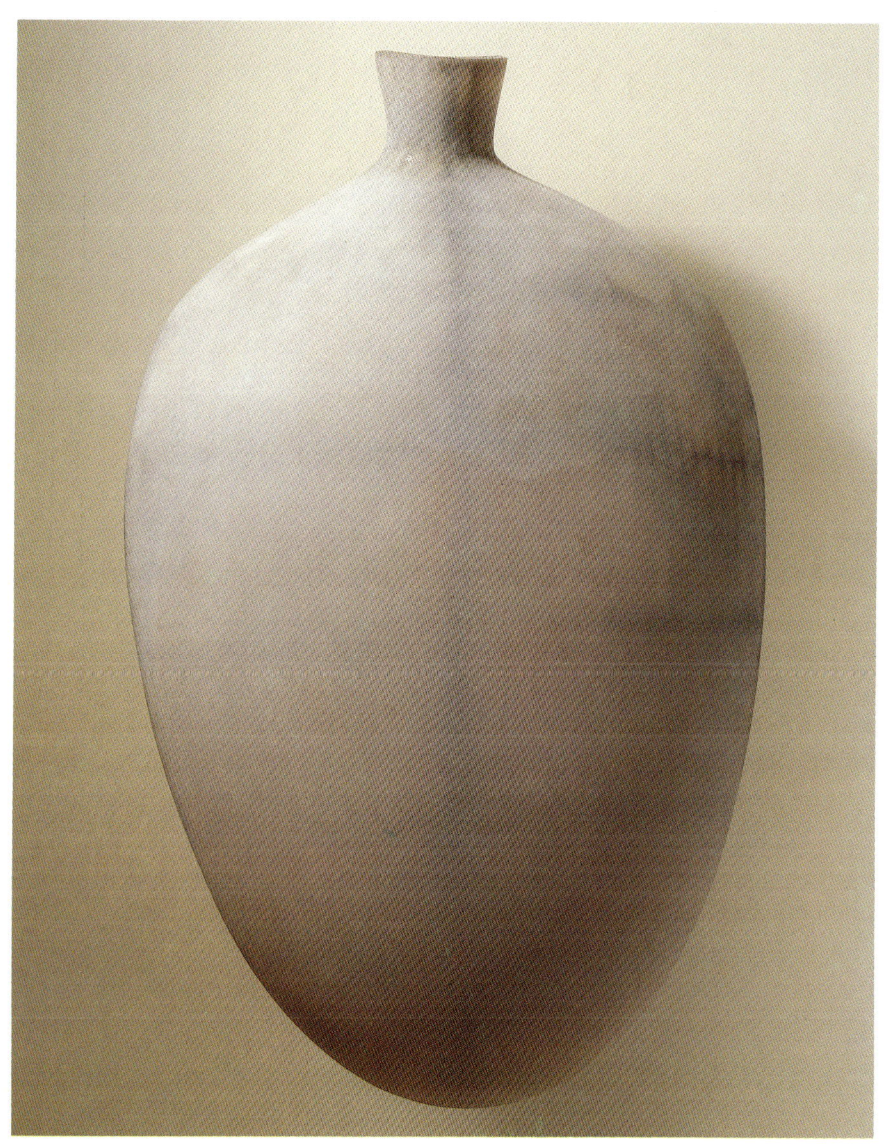

Bottleneck 1984-87, mixed media, 24 x 14 x 11 inches

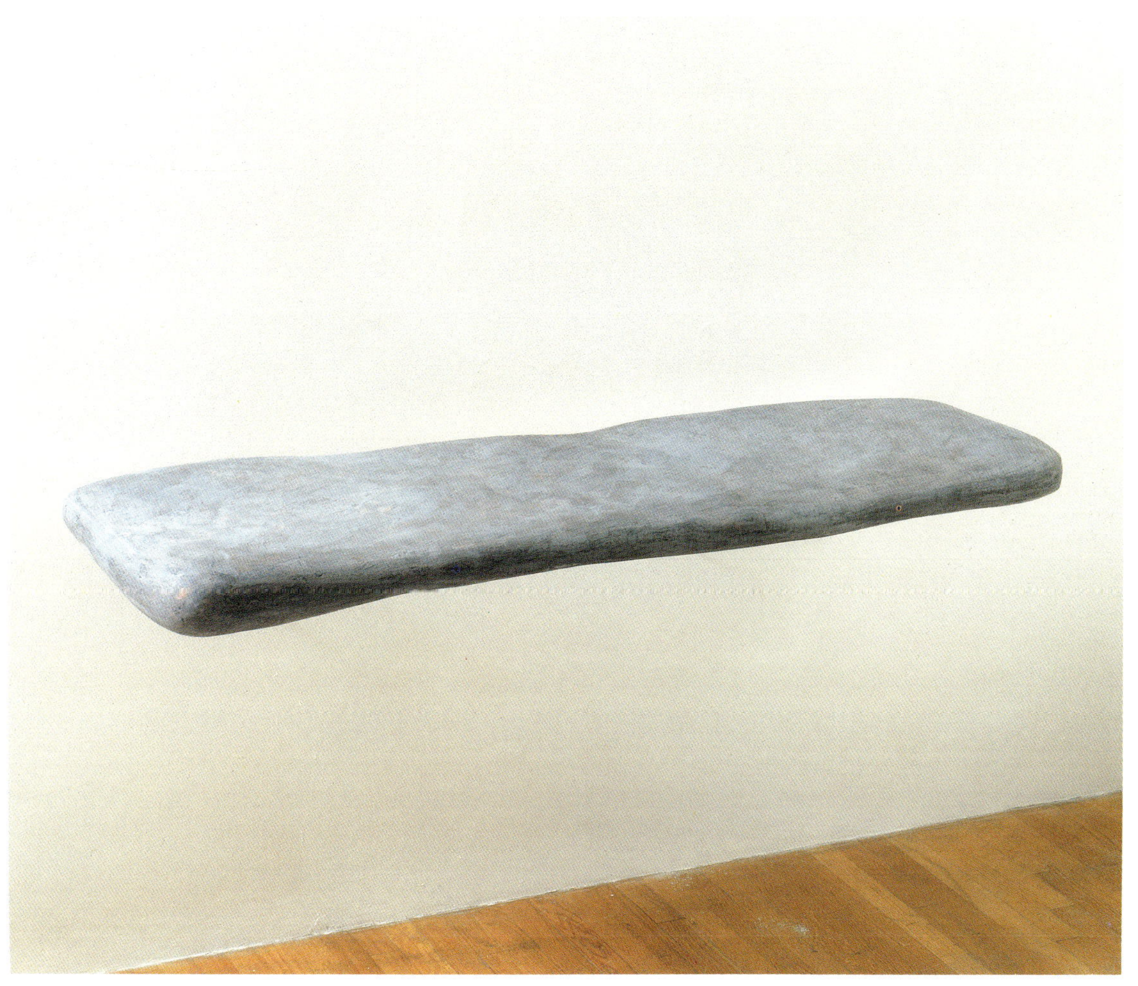

Greyfloater 1984-85, mixed media, 13 1/2 x 61 1/2 x 23 1/2 inches

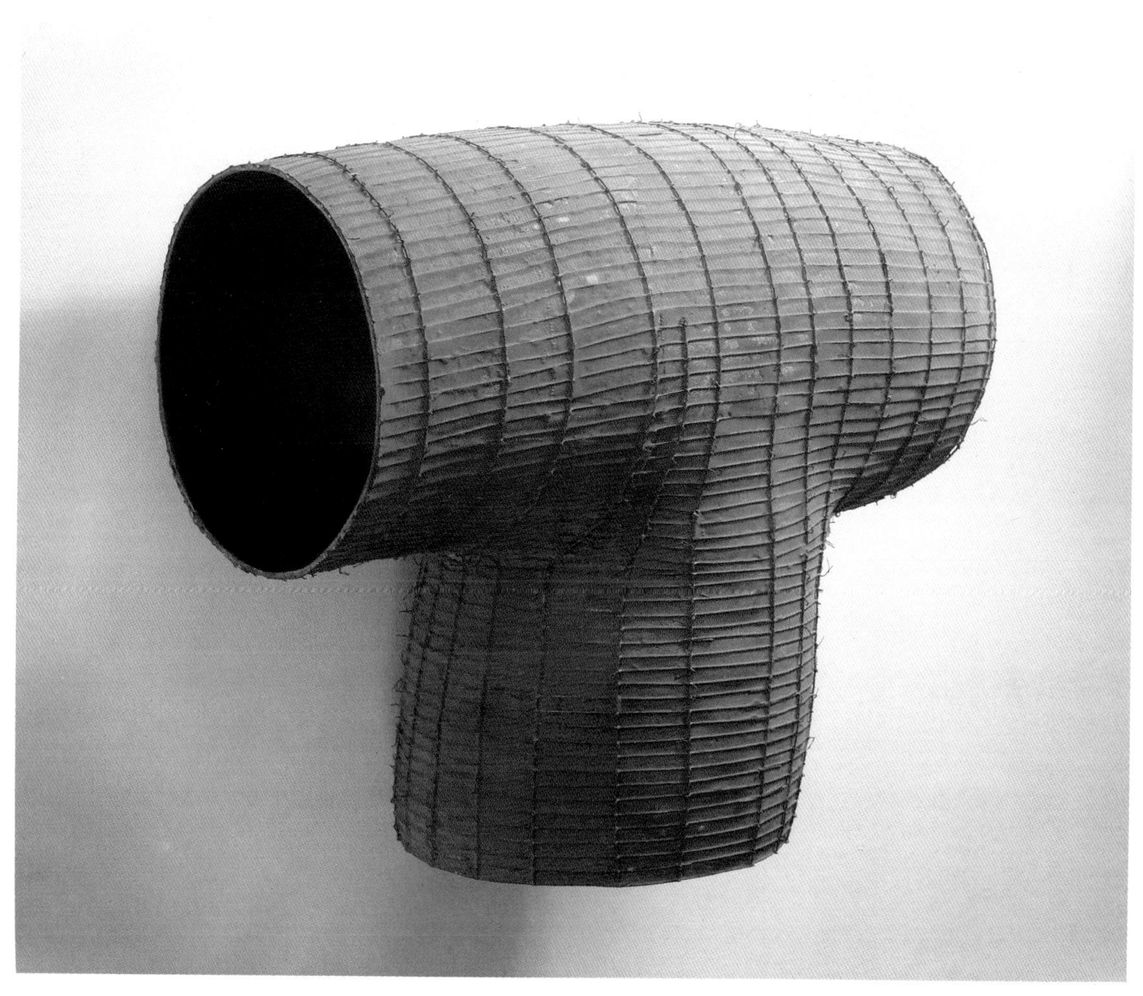

Bigblack T 1984-86, mixed media, 28 x 34 x 16 inches

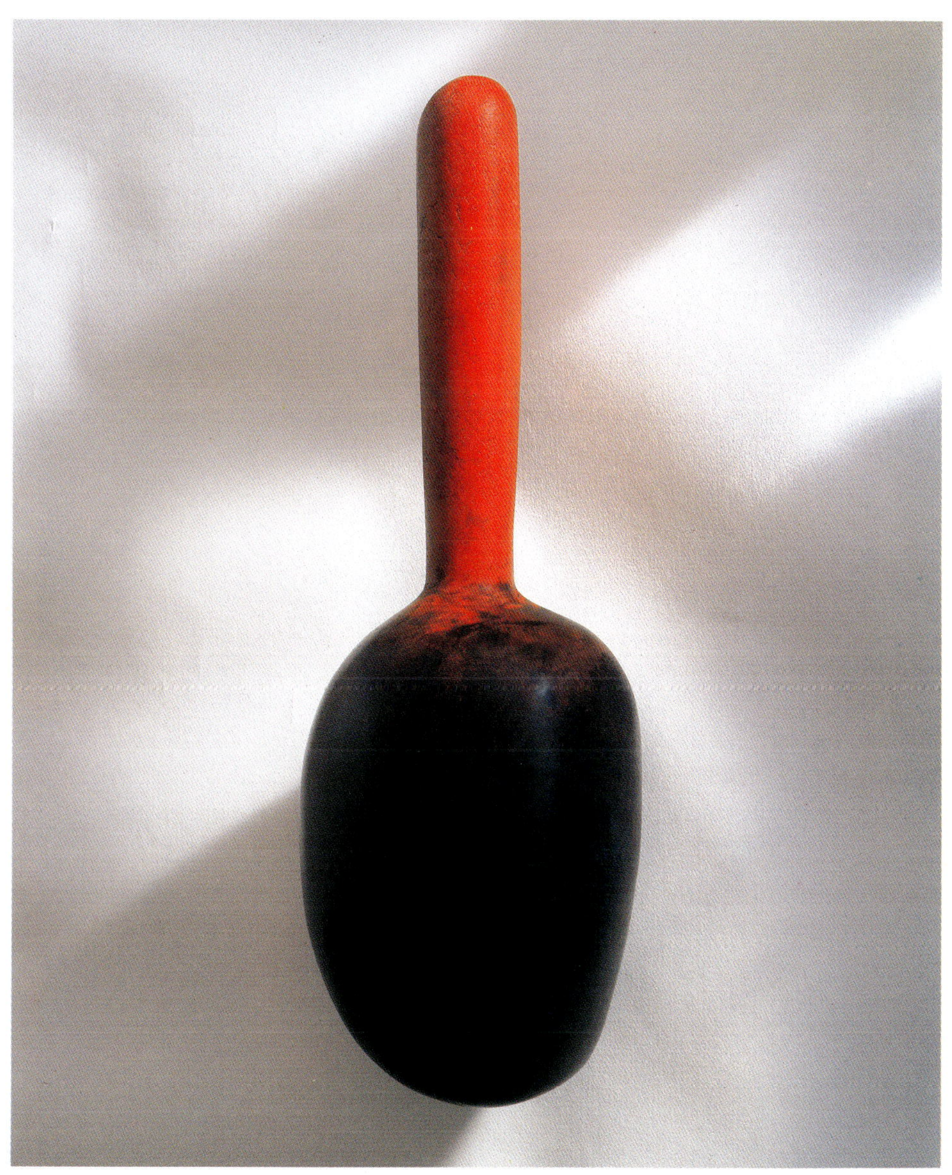

Peckerhead 1984-86, mixed media, 19 x 6 1/2 x 6 inches

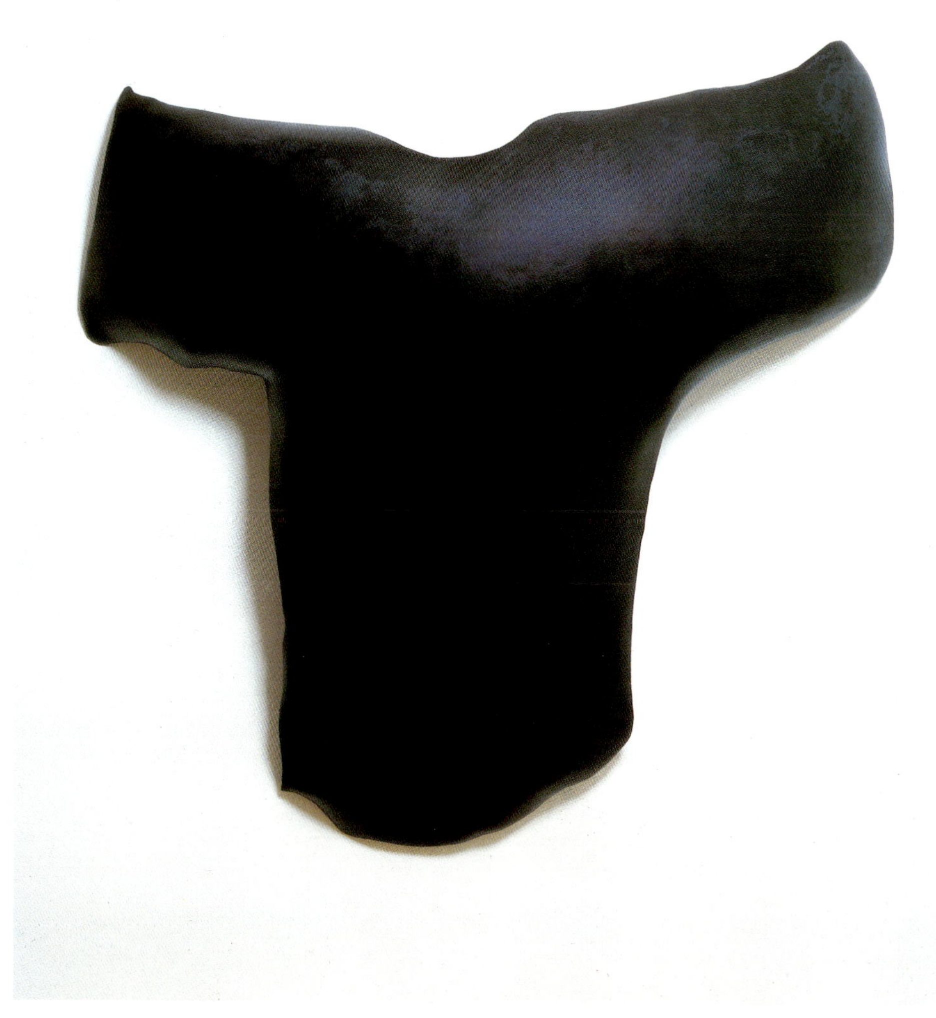

Blackshirt 1985, mixed media, 50 x 60 inches

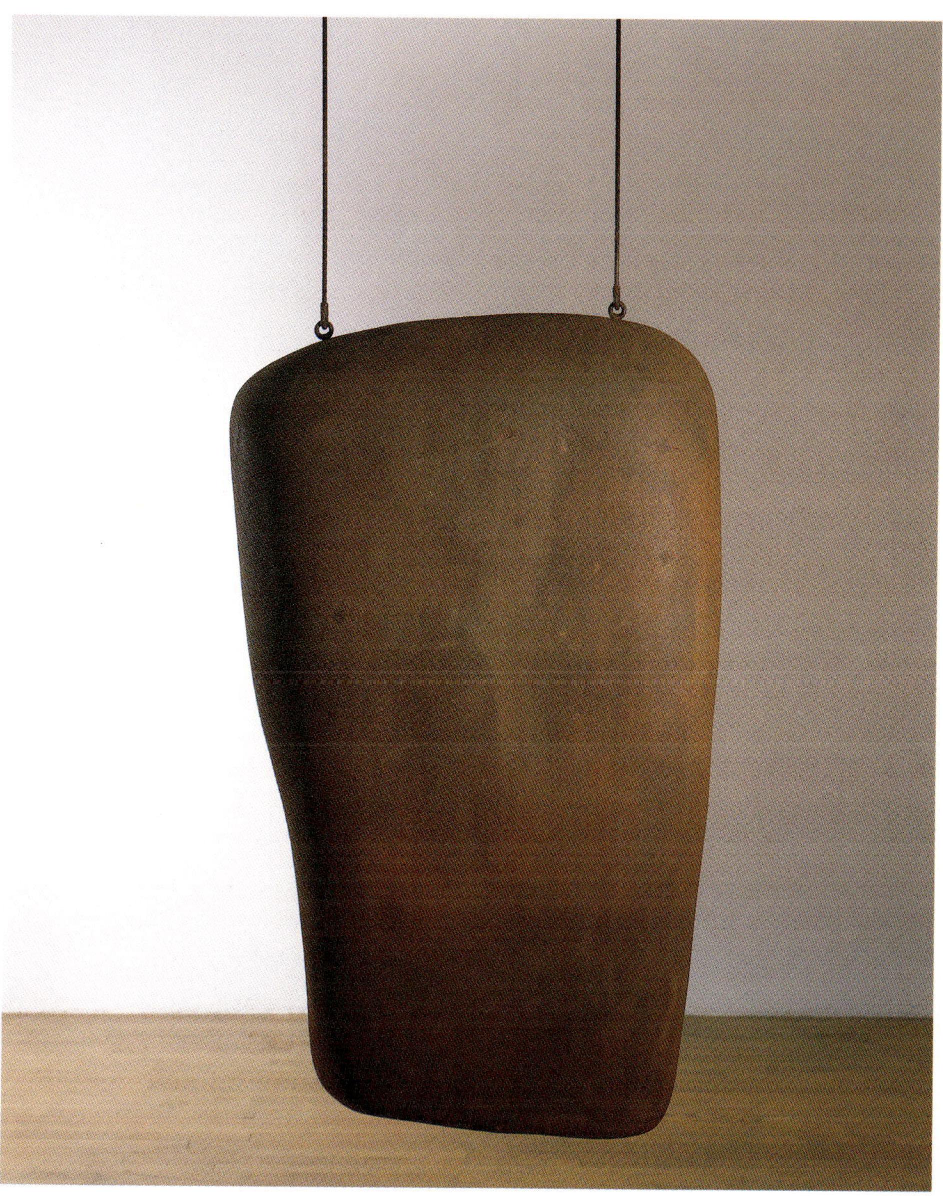

Ump 1984-86, cast iron, 43 x 26 x 13 inches

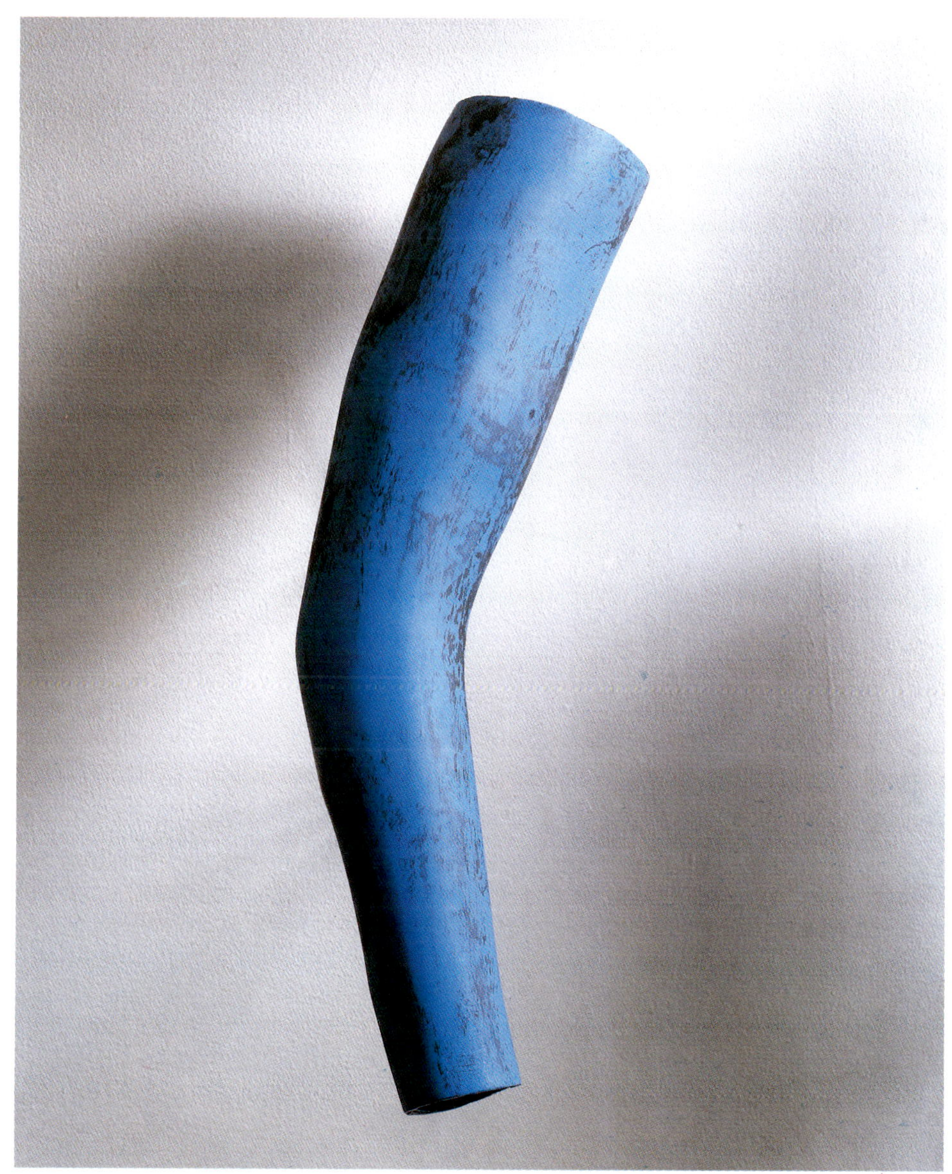

Bluearm 1984-86, mixed media, 22 x 4 1/2 x 17 inches

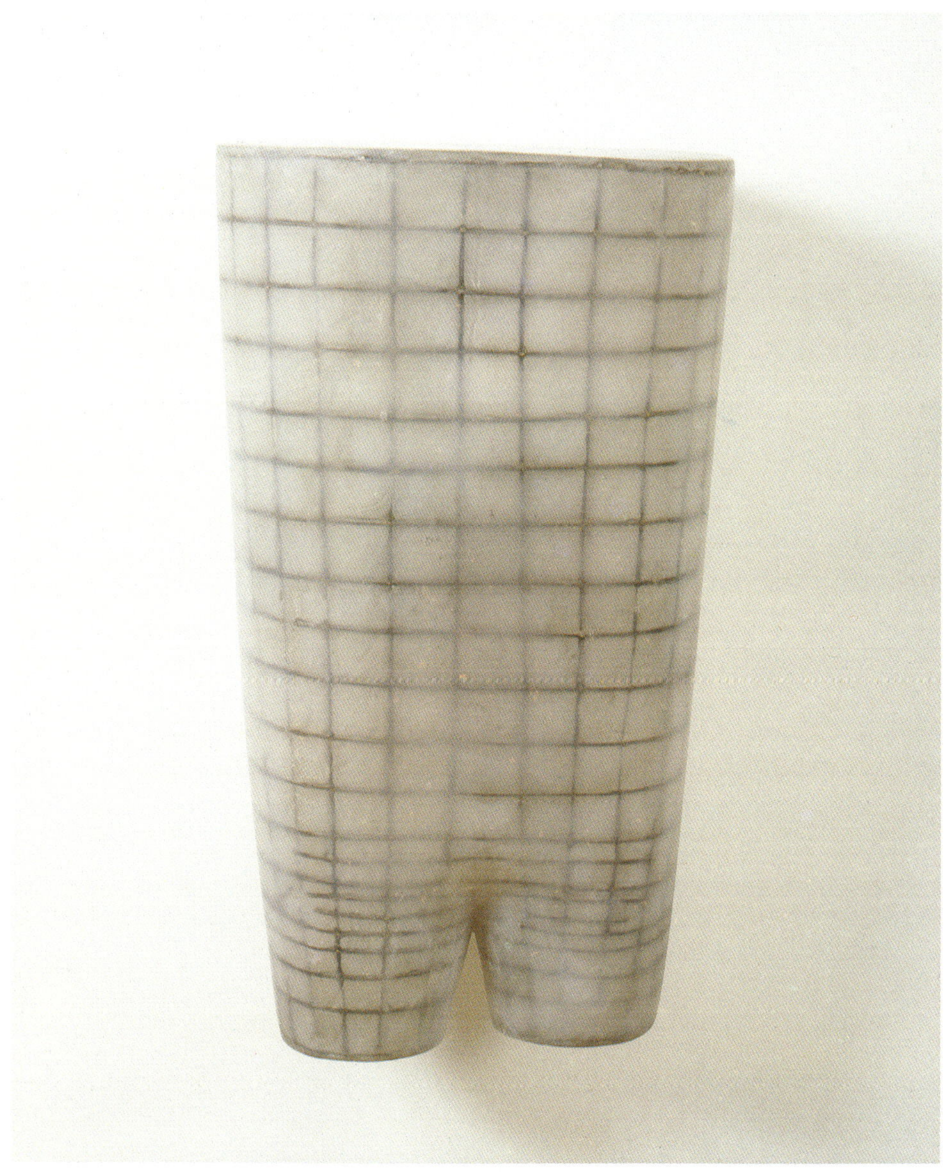

Tweedledee 1984-86, mixed media, 23 1/2 x 14 x 10 inches

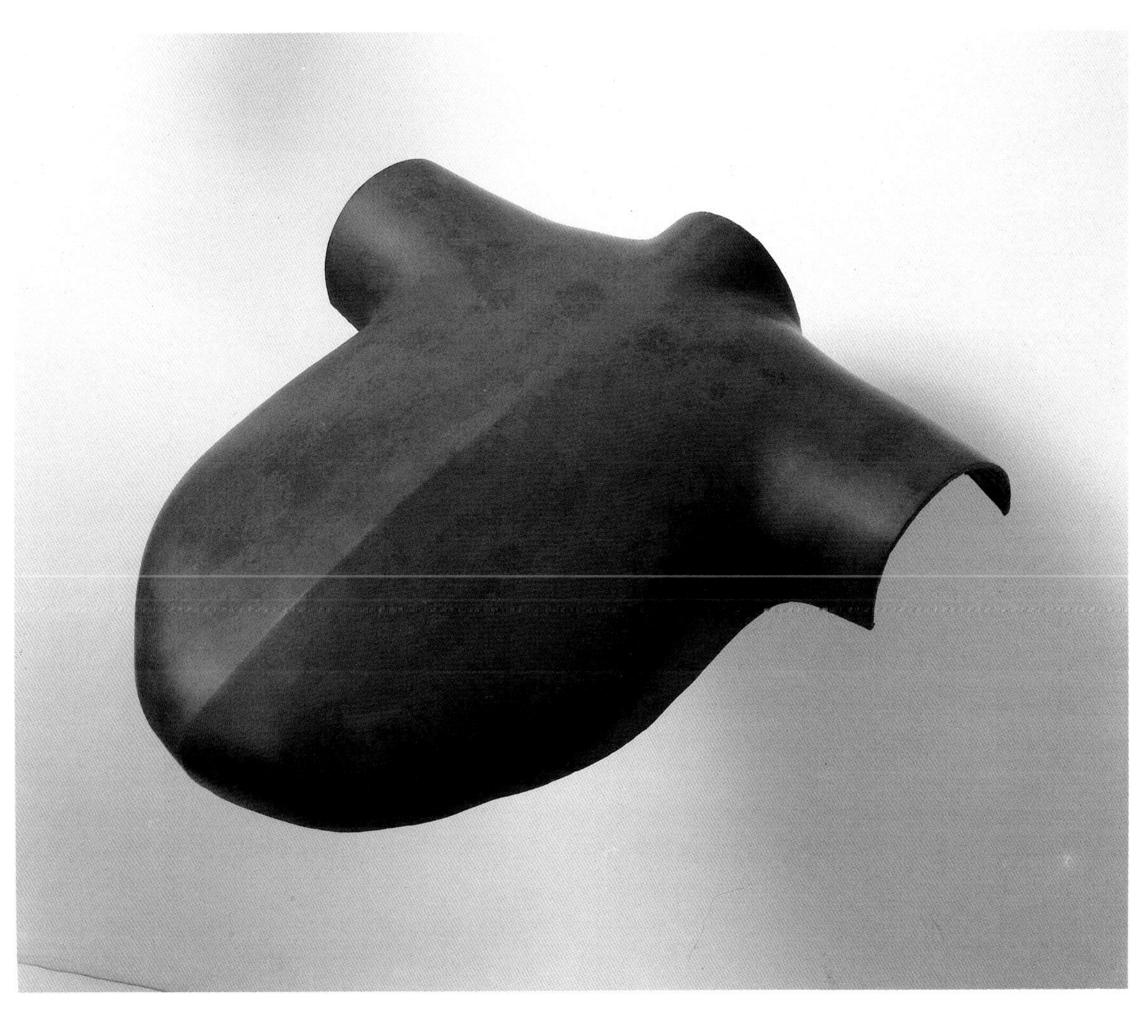

T Back 1985-86, mixed media, 31 x 31 x 6 inches

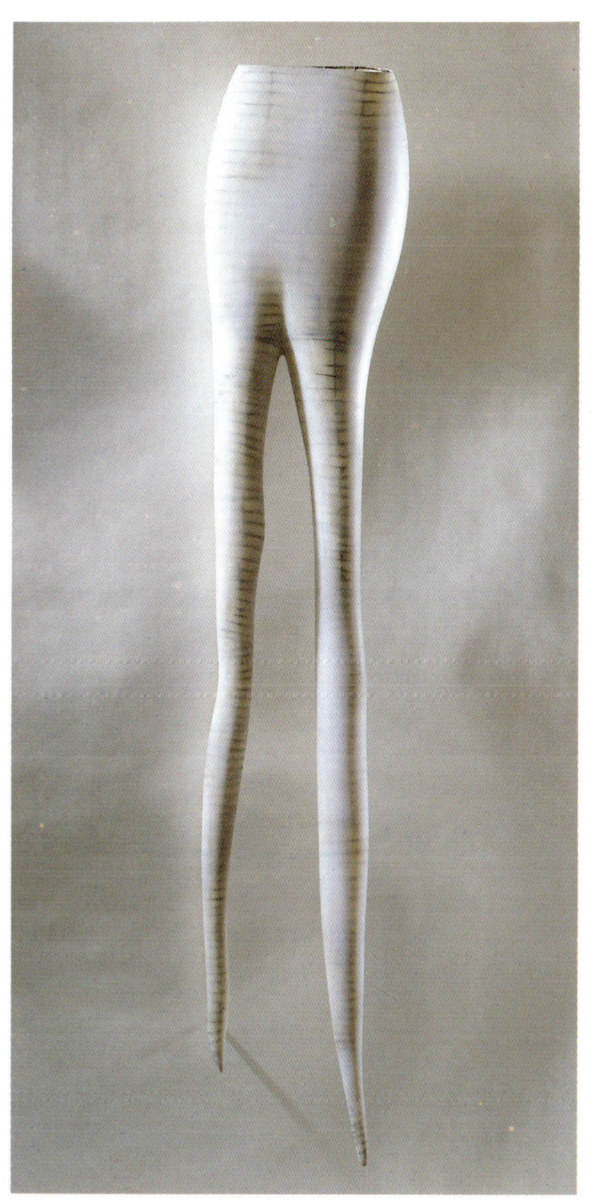

Pins 1983-87, mixed media, 61 x 12 1/4 x 5 1/2 inches

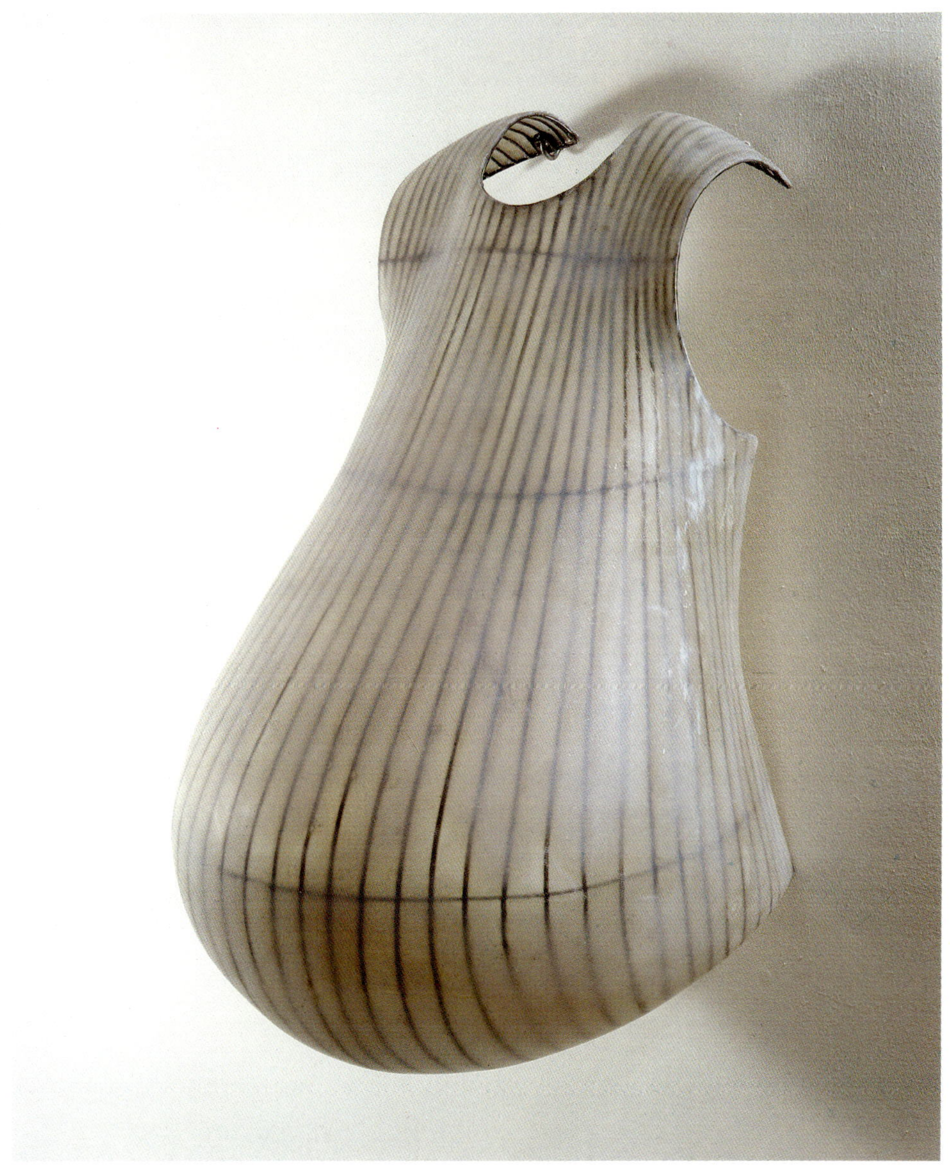

Clearbelly 1983, mixed media, 27 1/2 x 19 1/2 x 15 1/2 inches

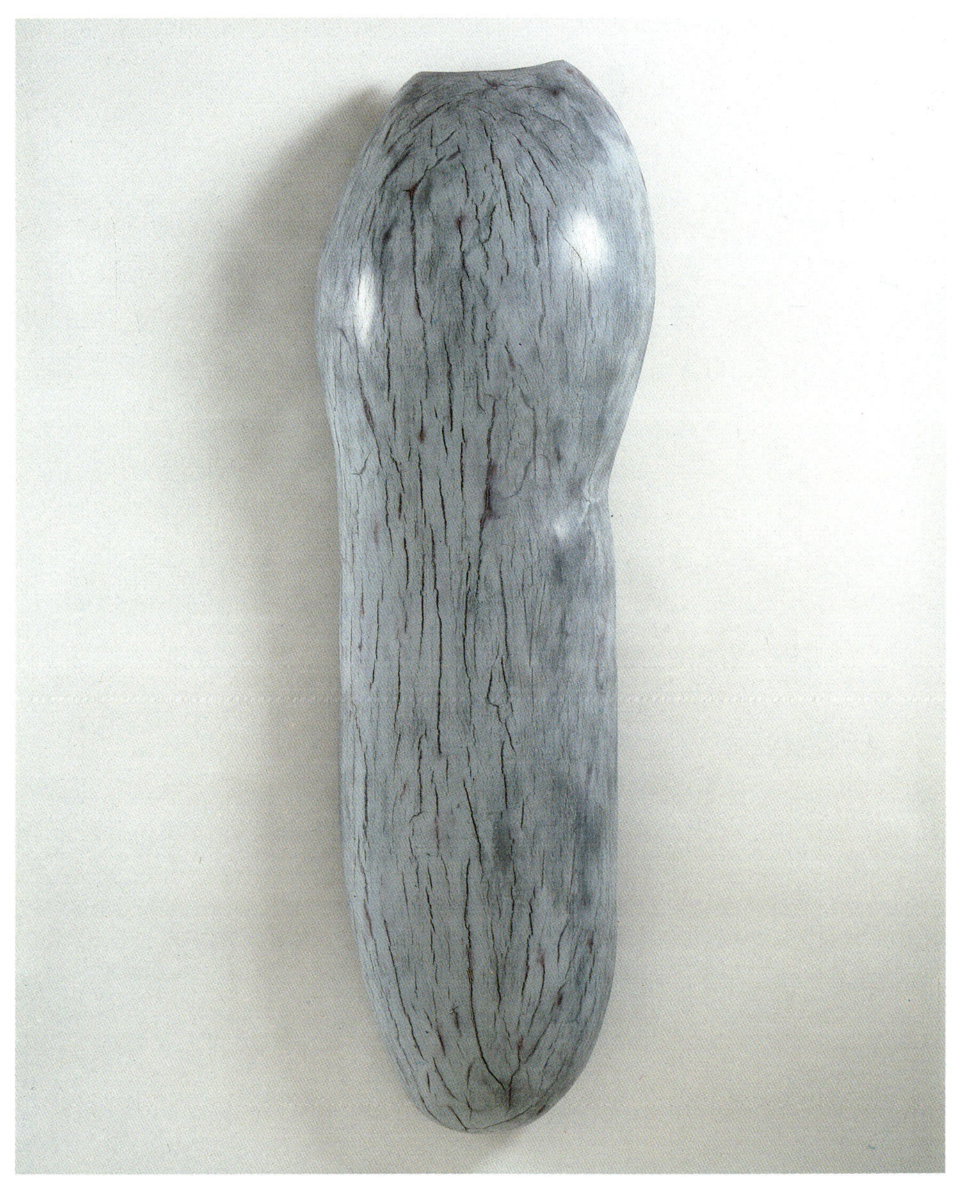

Greybone 1984-87, mixed media, 58 x 18 x 8 inches

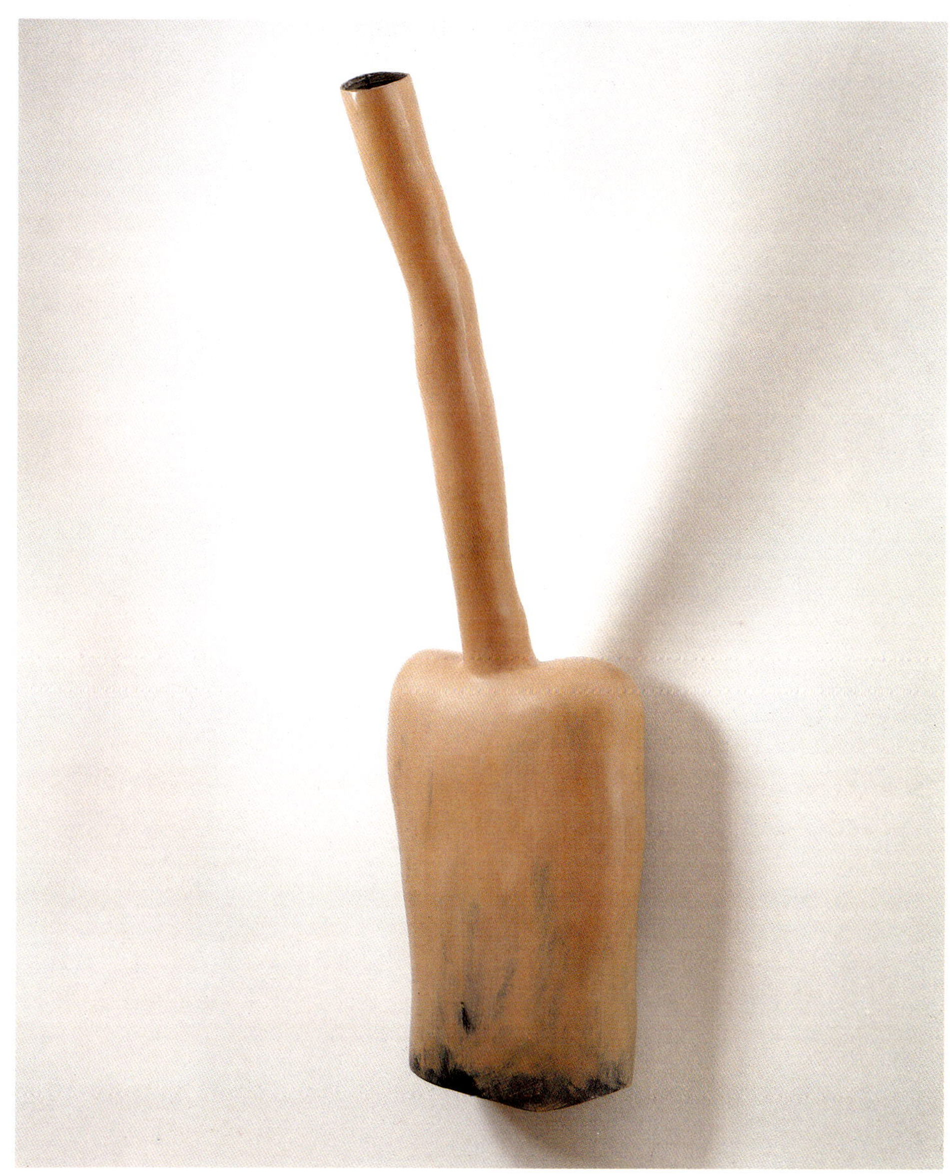

Gooseneck 1985-86, mixed media, 57 x 16 x 20 inches

EXHIBITION CHECKLIST

1

Whitepoint 1983-85, mixed media, 10 x 6 x 6 inches
Collection of Takashi Teramaye, Los Angeles

2

Redmantle 1984-86, mixed media, 9 x 16 1/2 inches
Collection of Takashi Teramaye, Los Angeles

3

Bluearm 1984-86, mixed media, 22 x 4 1/2 x 17 inches
Collection of Douglas S. Cramer, Los Angeles

4

Greyfloater 1984-85, mixed media, 13 1/2 x 61 1/2 x 23 1/2 inches
Courtesy of L.A. Louver, Venice, California

5

Farredpoints 1988, mixed media, 7 1/2 x 168 x 3 1/2 inches
Courtesy of L.A. Louver, Venice, California

6

Peckerhead 1984-86, mixed media, 19 x 6 1/2 x 6 inches
Collection of the artist

7

Twoarmstoolong 1986-88, cast bronze, 60 x 96 x 5 inches
Courtesy of L.A. Louver, Venice, California

8

Ironfloater 1984-86, cast iron, 6 x 65 x 22 inches
Collection of Anne Marie MacDonald, Tiburon, California

9

Bottleneck 1984-87, mixed media, 24 x 14 x 11 inches
Collection of Nancy and Bernie Kattler, Los Angeles

10

Ump 1984-86, cast iron, 43 x 26 x 13 inches
Collection of the Los Angeles County Museum of Art,
Modern and Contemporary Art Council Fund

11

Redwing 1983-85, mixed media, 70 x 60 x 7 inches
Collection of Dallas and David Price, Santa Monica, California

12

Blackwing 1985-86, mixed media, 6 x 73 x 22 inches
Robert A. Rowan Collection, Pasadena, California

13

T Back 1985-86, mixed media, 31 x 31 x 6 inches
Collection of Ann and Bill Harmsen, Los Angeles

14

Sleepwalker 1985-86, mixed media, 30 x 18 x 39 inches
Collection of Merry and Bill Norris, Los Angeles

15

Whitebeard 1986, mixed media, 38 x 20 x 9 inches
Collection of Vivi-Ann and Harold R. Blankstein, Los Angeles

16

Noarm 1985-86, mixed media, 45 x 16 x 8 1/2 inches
Collection of Vivi-Ann and Harold R. Blankstein, Los Angeles

17

Gooseneck 1985-86, mixed media, 57 x 16 x 20 inches
Courtesy of L.A. Louver, Venice, California

18

Whiteshirt 1987, mixed media, 38 x 60 x 4 inches
Collection of Jay Chiat, Los Angeles

19

Redshoulders 1987, mixed media, 30 1/4 x 35 x 6 1/4 inches
Collection of Charles C. and Sue K. Edwards, La Jolla, California

20

Simplecleartube 1983-87, mixed media, 4 x 126 x 5 inches
Courtesy of L.A. Louver, Venice, California

21

Bottom 1984-87, mixed media, 14 x 17 x 7 inches
Collection of Dr. Paul and Stacy Polydoran, Des Moines, Iowa

22

Clearbelly 1983-87, cast iron, 27 1/2 x 19 1/2 x 15 1/2 inches
Collection of The Edward R. Broida Trust, Los Angeles

23

Blackshirt 1985, mixed media, 50 x 60 inches
Collection of Merry and Bill Norris, Los Angeles

24

Pins 1983-87, mixed media, 61 x 12 1/4 x 5 1/2 inches
Courtesy of L.A. Louver, Venice, California

25

Slipper 1988, cast bronze, 4 x 34 inch diameter
Courtesy of L.A. Louver, Venice, California

26

Hammerhead 1984-86, mixed media, 63 x 21 x 9 inches
Collection of George and Gail Baril, Los Angeles

27

Greybone 1984-87, mixed media, approximately 58 x 18 x 8 inches
Collection of Mr. and Mrs. Harry Anderson, Palo Alto, California

28
Talkthrough 1983-86, mixed media, 6 1/2 x 7 3/4 x 9 1/2 inches
Collection of Craig W. Johnson, Los Angeles

29
Tweedledee 1984-86, mixed media, 23 1/2 x 14 x 10 inches
Collection of Robert and Mary Looker, Carpenteria, California

30
BigblackT 1984-86, mixed media, 28 x 34 x 16 inches
Collection of Michael Krichman and Leslie Simon, San Diego, California

31
Redleft 1985-86, mixed media, 6 x 73 x 22 inches
Collection of Roger and Amy Faxon, Los Angeles

32
Browntop 1984-85, mixed media, 28 inch diameter x 6 inches
Courtesy of L.A. Louver, Venice, California

33
Facein 1986, mixed media, 30 x 19 1/2 x 12 inches
Private collection, Courtesy of L.A. Louver, Venice, California

34
32th 1985-88, cast copper, 14 feet x 12 x 5 inches
Private collection, Courtesy of L.A. Louver, Venice, California

BIOGRAPHY

1951   Born, Troy, Ohio

Education

1973   B.A. Pomona College, Claremont, California
1974   Trade certifications
        Hobart School of Welding Technology, Troy Ohio
1979   M.F.A. University of California, Los Angeles

Teaching

1980-84 Lecturer, Otis Art Institute of the Parsons School
        of Design, Los Angeles
1981   Lecturer, Claremont Graduate School,
        Claremont, California
1985   Lecturer, University of Southern California

Awards/Grants

1977   Purchase Award – "Art in Public Places Exhibition"
        Cheney Cowles Memorial Art Museum,
        Spokane, Washington
1980   N.E.A., Artists Fellowship
1982   N.E.A., Artists Fellowship
1984   N.E.A., Artists Fellowship
1983   Commission for Outdoor Sculpture
        California Art Council
1985   Young Talent Award
        Los Angeles County Museum of Art
1987   Louis Comfort Tiffany Foundation Grant

DOCUMENTARY
FILM AND VIDEO

1979   Julie, K.C. "Peter Shelton – *SWEATHOUSE* and
        little principals," *New American Artist Series*,
        a video tape produced by Helicon video, Los Angeles.

1981   Shelton, Peter. *NECKWALL, footscreen, sleeper,*
        a 10 minute videotape, Los Angeles.

1984   Shelton, Peter. *MAJORJOINTS, hangers and squat,*
        a 6 minute videotape, Los Angeles.

        Shelton, Peter. *pipegut, waterseat and STANDSTILL,*
        a 3 minute videotape, Los Angeles.

1987   Shelton, Peter. *floatinghouse DEADMAN,* an 8 minute
        videotape, Los Angeles.

SELECTED
SOLO EXHIBITIONS
SITE WORKS AND
COMMISSIONS

1979   *SWEATHOUSE and little principals,* 111-element
        version, Wight Gallery, University of California,
        Los Angeles

1980   *BROWNROOMS 1977-78,* Los Angeles
        Contemporary Exhibitions, Inc. (L.A.C.E.)

        BIRDHOUSE, holecan, Chapman College,
        Orange, California. In conjunction with L.A.
        Institute of Contemporary Art "Architectural
        Sculpture" exhibition

        HEADROOM, footspace, Artpark, Lewiston,
        New York

1981   *NECKWALL, footscreen, sleeper,* Malinda Wyatt
        Gallery, Los Angeles

1982   *trunknuts, WHITEHEAD, floater,* Open Space
        Gallery, Victoria, British Columbia, Canada

        SWEATHOUSE and little principals, 150-element
        version, Santa Barbara Contemporary Arts
        Forum, California

        white, round, HEAD, Artists Space, New York

1983   *MAJORJOINTS, hangers and squat,* Center on
        Contemporary Art, Seattle, Washington

1984   *MAJORJOINTS, hangers and squat,* L.A. Louver
        and Malinda Wyatt Gallery, Los Angeles

        pipegut, waterseat and STANDSTILL, Portland
        Center for the Visual Arts, Oregon

1986   *floatinghouse, DEADMAN,* University of
        Massachusetts, Amhurst

        Peter Shelton: Recent Sculpture, L.A. Louver,
        Venice, California

1987   *floatinghouse, DEADMAN,* Wight Art Gallery,
        University of California, Los Angeles

        TUB, tubes and pipes, HARDSTRETCH, droop,
        Whitney Museum of American Art.

1988　*STRETCH, spread,* The Lannan Museum,
Lake Worth, Florida

BLACKVAULT, falloffstone, Walker Art Center,
Minneapolis, Minnesota

SELECTED GROUP EXHIBITIONS

1977　*Art in Public Places,* Cheney Cowles
Memorial Museum, Spokane, Washington

1980　*Sculpture 1980,* The Maryland Institute,
College of Art, Baltimore, Maryland

*Maquettes and Models – Art with Architectural
Concerns,* Los Angeles Municipal Art Gallery

Architectural Sculpture – History and Documents,
Los Angeles Institute of Contemporary Art

1981　*Divola, Picot, Shelton,* Libra Gallery, Claremont
Graduate School of Fine Arts,
Claremont, California

With More than One Sense, Los Angeles County
Museum of Art, California

The Intimate Object, Downtown Gallery,
Los Angeles

1982　*Forgotten Dimension,* Fresno Art Center,
Fresno, California

1983　*Une Expérience Muséographique: Echange Entre
Artistes 1931-1982 Pologne – U.S.A.,*
Musée D'Art Moderne de la Ville de Paris and
The Ulster Museum, Belfast, Ireland

Public Comments, Center on Contemporary Art,
Seattle, Washington

1984　*Constructed Metal: Modern Sculpture,*
College of Creative Studies, University of
California, Santa Barbara, California

Aperto '84, The Venice Biennale, Venice, Italy

1985　*Anniottanta,* Museum of Modern Art,
Bologna, Italy

1987　*Sculpture and Drawings by Sculptors,*
L.A. Louver, Venice, California

California Figurative Sculpture, Palm Springs
Desert Museum, California

Invitational Exhibition, Curt Marcus Gallery,
New York

Avant-Garde in the Eighties, Los Angeles County
Museum of Art

1988　*Elements: Five Installations,* Whitney Museum
of American Art, New York

Abstract Expressions: Recent Sculpture,
Lannan Museum, Lake Worth, Florida

Striking Distance, The Museum of Contemporary
Art, Los Angeles

Sculpture: Inside and Outside, Walker
Art Center, Minneapolis, Minnesota

SELECTED BIBLIOGRAPHY

1977　*Art in Public Places,* Cheney Cowles Memorial
Art Museum, Spokane, Washington.

1980　*Sculpture 1980,* Maryland Institute,
College of Art, illus.

Fahr, Barry. "Enigmatic Architecture," *Artweek,*
vol. II, no. 23, June 21, 1980, illus.

Huntington, Richard. "Artpark Does its Best to
Get Rid of the Middleman," *Buffalo Courier
Express,* July 13, 1980, illus.

Branche, Bill. "Artpark Sculpture Evokes
Simplicity, Strength," *Niagara Gazette,*
August 10, 1980.

Larson, Kay. "Is There a Crimp in the Beauty
Parlor," *The Village Voice,* September 10-16, 1980.

Lippard, Lucy. "The Inside Picture from the
Outside," *Architectural Sculpture – Projects,*
Los Angeles Institute of Contemporary Art,
1980, p. 25, 87, illus.

Turner, Richard. "Peter Shelton," *Architectural
Sculpture – Projects,* Los Angeles, Institute
of Contemporary Art, 1980, pp. 29-31, illus.

Muchnic, Suzanne. "Sprawling Sculptures,"
The Los Angeles Times Calendar, November 2, 1980.

Brodhead, Wendy. "Protection and Entrapment,"
Artweek, vol. II, no. 39, November 22, 1980, illus.

1981　Knight, Christopher. "Your Place or Shelton's,"
Herald Examiner, May 10, 1981, p. E3, illus.

Artpark 1980, Visual Arts,
Lewiston, New York, illus.

Schipper, Merle. "Peter Shelton's Places and
Spaces," *Images and Issues,* vol. I, no. 4,
Spring 1981, pp. 24-25, illus.

Blaine, Michael. "Formalist Shelter," *Artweek,*
vol. 12, no. 18, May 16, 1981, illus.

Wortz, Melinda. "A Tropical Sleeper," *Artnews*, October 1981, p. 189.

Lewinson, David. "With Another Sense," *Artweek*, vol. 12, no. 37, November 7, 1981, illus.

1982   Shelton, Peter. "NECKWALL, footscreen, sleeper," *Dreamworks*, Spring 1982, vol. 3, pp. 203-207, cover illus.

Wilson, Raymond L. "Small Metaphors," *Artweek*, vol.13, no. 17, p.4, May 1, 1982, illus.

Une Expérience Muséographique: Echange Entre Artistes 1931-1982 Pologne – U.S.A., Musée D'Art Moderne de la Ville de Paris, 1982, illus.

Knight, Christopher. *Peter Shelton – Sculpture*, Open Space Gallery, Victoria, British Columbia, 1982, illus.

Amos, Robert. "Peter Shelton at Open Space Gallery," *Vanguard*, vol. II, nos. 8 & 9, October/November 1982, pp. 27-28, illus.

Timberman, Marcy. "Peter Shelton: The Power of the Ordinary," *Artweek*, vol. 13, no. 40, November 27, 1982, cover, p.16, illus.

Hicks, Mary. "Peter Shelton at Contemporary Arts Forum, Santa Barbara," *Images and Issues*, vol. 3, no. 5, March/April 1983, pp. 63-64, illus.

1983   Wortz, Melinda. "Peter Shelton – Contemporary Arts Forum, Santa Barbara: 'SWEATHOUSE and little principals 1977-82,'" *Artnews*, May 1983, pp. 133-136, illus.

Donnelly, Micky. "An Artistic Conversation 1931-1982: Poland/U.S.A., Ulster Museum, Belfast," *Circa*, Belfast, March-April, 1983.

Smallwood, Lyn. "COCA's 'Public Comments:' an old warehouse for new art," *The Weekly*, Seattle, Dec. 7-14, 1983, pp. 40-41, illus.

Fallon, Brian. "Polish-U.S. exhibition at Ulster Museum," *Irish Times*, Belfast, March 1, 1983.

Hackett, Regina. "Public Comments," *Seattle Post- Intelligencer*, Seattle, December 3, 1983, p. C12.

1984   Colpitt, Francis. *Constructed Metal: Modern Sculpture*, College of Creative Studies, University of California, Santa Barbara, 1984, illus.

Glowen, Ron. "Morphology and Material," *Artweek*, vol. 15, no. 21, May 26, 1984, p. 5, illus.

Groot, Paul. "Closed Quotes," *Artforum*, September 1984, p. 107.

Gendel, Milton. "Report from Venice, Cultured Pearls at the Biennale," *Art in America*, September 1984, p. 51, illus.

Di Biumo, Giuseppe Panza. "La Biennale," *Domus*, Arte Section, August 1984, p. 72.

Schipper, Merle. "MAJORJOINTS, hangers and squat," *Arts and Architecture*, Winter 1984, pp. 15-16, illus. vol. 3, no. 2.

Gardner, Colin. "Peter Shelton at L.A. Louver and Malinda Wyatt Galleries," *Images and Issues*, July/August 1984, p. 41, illus.

Caroli, Flavio. "Pittura Veloce, Post-Astrazione E Post-Naturalismo," *Catalogo Generale 1984*, *La Biennale di Venezia*, Venice, Italy, p. 201, 213 illus.

1985   Muchnic, Suzanne. "2 Sculptors Earn Young Talent Prize," *The Los Angeles Times Calendar*, June 24, 1985, pp. 1-5.

Cabutti, Lucio. "Uno Squardo Sugli Anni Ottanta-Bologna E Altre Citta," *Arte*, Grandi Mostre Section, July/August 1985, p. 26, illus.

Pietrantonio, Giacinto Di. "I Luoghi Mobili Dell'Indefinito: Neoinformale, Postastrazione E Neomonimalismo," *Anniottanta*, Milano, Italy, pp. 123, 152, 161, illus.

Drohojowska, Hunter. "The Prize," *Los Angeles Herald Examiner*, June 25, 1985, p. C3, illus.

Bodino, di Maristella. "I Dupotutto," *Epoca*, Milano, Italy, July 19, 1985, pp. 42-51, illus.

1986   Wright, Patricia. "A house levitates," *The Hampshire Gazette*, Springfield, Mass., February 25, 1986.

Holland, Laura. "Peter Shelton: U. Mass, Amherst," *Art New England: A Resource for the Visual Arts*, March 1986, p.10, illus.

1987   Mallinson, Constance. "Peter Shelton at L.A. Louver," *Art in America*, February 1987, p. 154-155, illus.

Knight, Christopher. "'Deadman' exhibit exudes life," *Los Angeles Herald Examiner*, February 26, 1987, p. B7, illus.

Bijvoet, Marga. "Engaging the Viewer/Participant," *Artweek*, February 28, 1987, p. 1, illus.

Anderson, Michael. "Pick of the Week," *L.A. Weekly*, February 27 – March 5, 1987, illus.

Wakefield, Sanford Suzan. "Shelton's installation: 'light, blond and buoyant'," *The Outlook*, February 27, 1987, illus.

Bulmer, Marge. "Peter Shelton's 'floatinghouse DEADMAN,'" *Reader*, February 27, 1987, illus.

Muchnic, Suzanne. "Exploring a House that Floats," *The Los Angeles Times*, March 2, 1987, illus.

Baltierra, Miguel. "floatinghouse DEADMAN," *L.A. Architect*, March 1987, p. 7, illus.

Gardner, Colin. "Peter Shelton – UCLA Wight Art Gallery," *Artforum*, May 1987, p. 158, illus.

Drohojowska, Hunter. "The Artists Who Matter: L.A.'s New Scene Makes History," *Antiques and Fine Art*, June 1987, p. 49-55, illus.

Fox, Howard. *Avant Garde in the Eighties*, Exhibition Catalogue, Los Angeles County Museum of Art, Los Angeles 1987.

Zakian, Michael. *California Figurative Sculpture*, Exhibition Catalogue, Palm Springs Desert Museum, California 1987, illus.

Comi, Enrico. "Peter Shelton," *Spazio Umano*, Milano, 2/1987, illus.

Clothier, Peter. "Peter Shelton," *Artnews*, Studios Sect., September 1987, p. 82-83, illus.

1988   Levin, Kim. "Elements: Five Installations," *The Village Voice*, New York, January 5, 1988, p. 84, illus.

Monaghan, Kathleen. *Elements: Five Installations*, Whitney Museum of American Art, New York, 1987, illus.

Brenson, Michael. "A Transient Art Form with Staying Power," *The New York Times*, January 10, 1988, pp. 33-36.

Clearwater, Bonnie. *Abstract Expressions: Recent Sculpture*, Exhibition Catalogue, The Lannan Museum, Lake Worth, Florida, 1987, illus.

Brenson, Michael. "Fossilization Evolved into a Modern Metaphor," *The New York Times*, January 31, 1988.

Friedman, Martin. *Sculpture Inside Outside*, Exhibition Catalogue, Walker Art Center, Minneapolis, Minnesota, 1988, illus.

This exhibition is funded through the generous support
of the
Anna K. Meredith Endowment Fund
and the
Lannan Foundation

This first edition of
PETER SHELTON: WAXWORKS
is limited to three thousand copies
contents copyright Des Moines Art Center 1988
design by Jack Woody, Twelvetrees Press
typography composed by Scott Smith
exhibition curator Cornelia H. Butler
photographs by Thomas P. Vinetz unless otherwise indicated
Library of Congress catalogue number 88-070611
ISBN 0-914615-4-3

Exhibition
DES MOINES ART CENTER
24 September – 13 November 1988

LA JOLLA MUSEUM OF CONTEMPORARY ART
7 April – 4 June 1989

DES MOINES ART CENTER
4700 Grand Avenue
Des Moines, Iowa 50312-2099